WHAT A KICK

HOW A CLUTCH WORLD CUP WIN PROPELLED WOMEN'S SOCCER

by Emma Carlson Berne

Content Adviser: Tracy Noonan
U.S. Women's National Team goalkeeper (1996–1999) and
founding member, Women's United Soccer Association

COMPASS POINT BOOKS
a capstone imprint

Compass Point Books are published by Capstone,
1710 Roe Crest Drive, North Mankato, Minnesota 56003
www.mycapstone.com

Editor: Catherine Neitge
Designers: Tracy Davies McCabe and Catherine Neitge
Media Researcher: Eric Gohl
Library Consultant: Kathleen Baxter
Production Specialist: Lori Barbeau

Image Credits
AP Photo: Reed Saxon, 29; Corbis: George Tiedemann, 17, 19, 26; Getty Images: AFP/Hector Mata, 40, 48, AFP/Roberto Schmidt, cover, 13, 36, 44, 46, AFP/Timothy A. Clary, 23, AFP/Tommy Cheng, 56 (bottom), Al Bello, 58 (top), Allsport/Jamie Squire, 31, Bob Thomas, 18, 27, 57 (left), Bongarts/Henri Szwarc, 51, David Cannon, 28, Elsa, 34, The LIFE Images Collection/Will Mcintyre, 15, *Miami Herald*/Joe Rimkus Jr., 59 (top), Ronald Martinez, 58 (bottom), *Sports Illustrated*/Heinz Kluetmeier, 11, *Sports Illustrated*/John W. McDonough, 7, 22, 25, *Sports Illustrated*/Peter Read Miller, 33, 41, 55, *Sports Illustrated*/Robert Beck, 35, 47, Vincent Laforet, 9, 43, *The Washington Post*/Rich Lipski, 38; Newscom: ABACA/PA Photos/Ridley Vaughn, 59 (bottom), dpa/picture-alliance/Oliver Berg, 56 (top), KRT/Nuccio Dinuzzo, 6, 21, Reuters/Gary Hershorn, 37, Reuters/Rick Wilking, 5, SIPA/Red Bull/Mirja Geh, 24, UPI Photo Service/Jim Ruymen, 10, 49, UPI Photo Service/Joel Rennich, 57 (right), ZUMA Press/Andrew Chin, 53

Library of Congress Cataloging-in-Publication Data
Cataloging-in-publication information is on file with the Library of Congress.
ISBN 978-0-7565-5293-0 (library binding)
ISBN 978-0-7565-5297-8 (paperback)
ISBN 978-0-7565-5301-2 (ebook PDF)

Printed in the United States of America, in Stevens Point Wisconsin.
092015   009222WZS16

TABLEOFCONTENTS

ChapterOne
FIVE KICKS, FIVE CHANCES

The field was blistering hot that day at the Rose Bowl stadium in Pasadena, California. Some members of the U.S. Women's National Soccer Team lay on the turf, towels draped over their necks, as trainers massaged their aching legs. Others stood in huddles, pouring water over their heads and bouncing back and forth to keep their legs loose. They were all exhausted.

It was July 10, 1999, and the thermometer measured 105 degrees Fahrenheit (41 degrees Celsius). It was the final game of the 1999 Women's World Cup, the ultimate in women's soccer. Sixteen teams had participated in the final tournament over the last 21 days. Now, in the scorching summer heat of the final match, the last two teams had run the field for 90 minutes and two 15-minute overtimes. The score was 0-0. And the U.S. athletes on the field were like hounds at a hunt. They were going to capture the World Cup, no matter what.

They were facing China, a powerful opponent, which had beaten them three months earlier in an exhibition game. But the Chinese players were tired too. Sun Wen, the Chinese forward, had feet full of blisters. "We were all exhausted," U.S. forward Tiffeny Milbrett later recalled. "I don't think as much physically as mentally. I was surprised by how tired I thought China was too. … Technique was breaking down. You just have to fight through it. You just have to battle."

U.S. forward Tiffeny Milbrett (16) was chased down the field during the second half of the Women's World Cup final game.

Two overtimes, and no one had scored. The game was going into a dreaded phase: penalty kicks. The players hated them. Five kicks for each team. One shooter versus the opponent's goalkeeper. The team that puts more kicks past the goalkeeper wins. It's as simple as that. But penalty kicks say almost nothing about the physical skills of a player. A decent amateur can kick the ball past even a good goalkeeper. Penalty kicks are all about mind games.

Kristine Lilly battled for the ball. She would be one of the five shootout kickers for the Americans.

All about concentration, outwitting the goalkeeper, and keeping your mind tightly focused.

Who would kick for the American team? Lauren Gregg, the U.S. assistant coach, wrote down four names: team captain Carla Overbeck, defender Joy Fawcett, midfielder Kristine Lilly, and superstar forward Mia Hamm. There were two possibilities for the fifth spot, co-captain Julie Foudy and midfielder and defender Brandi Chastain. If the score was still tied after four kicks per team, the fifth could win the World Cup. They would need a clutch

Co-captain Julie Foudy, who played on four World Cup teams, was the possible fifth kicker.

performer. Someone who could handle the pressure of being the possible decider. Someone who could surprise China's goalkeeper.

Gregg walked over to Chastain. She wasn't the obvious pick. She had become predictable kicking with her right leg, with the ball going to the goalkeeper's right. Chastain had missed more than half of her penalty kicks that year. But she had a special skill: she could shoot with either foot. She could kick left-footed if she had to. Maybe most important, she had the guts to try it in a World Cup final.

Chastain was lying facedown on the turf with her eyes closed, fighting a leg cramp. "Do you want a kick?" Gregg asked. Chastain said she did. Then Gregg suggested a new tactic: "Kick it with your left foot." Chastain agreed. And just like that, the decision had been made. The list was complete.

The United States was watching. The world was watching. Little girls, teenage boys, fans in face paint, body paint, USA shirts and hats—soccer fans of every type packed the Rose Bowl. Four years before, in 1995, the Americans had played in the World Cup semifinals in Sweden in front of 3,000 people. Before the 1999 World Cup finals, that many fans showed up just to watch practice. The players were so mobbed, they needed police escorts just to get off the field. Just 21 days before, the United States had hammered Denmark 3-0 in front of nearly 79,000 screaming fans. Now 90,185 people filled the stadium. Another 40 million watched on TV in the United States. One billion people watched worldwide. It was the biggest event in the history of women's sports. And it had come down to five kicks.

The ball was placed on a dot 12 yards (11 meters) from the goal. The teams would alternate kicks. Chinese player Xie Huilin was up first. Briana Scurry, the American goalkeeper, danced nervously in the box, but Xie shot easily past her into the upper left corner of the net. Goal for the Chinese.

It was the biggest event in the history of women's sports. And it had come down to five kicks.

Defender Carla Overbeck leaped high in the air after her successful penalty kick.

Carla Overbeck, the team captain, was the first American kicker. She jogged up to the ball, the picture of casual confidence. She was even chewing gum. The entire stadium held its breath. Overbeck kicked. Chinese goalkeeper Gao Hong lunged for the ball—the wrong way. The ball sailed into the net, and the stadium exploded in cheers.

Chinese player Qiu Haiyan shot next—scored. Joy Fawcett, American defender—scored. The tension in

Superstar Mia Hamm scored a penalty kick beyond the reach of goalkeeper Gao Hong.

the stadium was rising. The score was tied 2-2. On the next penalty kick, Scurry blocked Chinese player Liu Ying's shot. The dive to block the shot was so explosive that for three months, Scurry thought she'd torn an abdominal muscle.

Two more Americans shot and scored: Kristine Lilly and Mia Hamm. Zhang Ouying and Sun Wen had also scored for the Chinese. The score was tied, 4-4. Chastain was up. If she scored a goal, the Americans would win the World Cup 5-4. If she missed, a new round of kicks would begin.

Chastain later said all the sounds became muffled when she set the ball on the mark. Still, Chastain recalled,

THE ART OF SPORTS PHOTOGRAPHY

Sports photographer Bill Frakes shot from the sidelines during an NFL game in Tampa, Florida.

Sports photographers are also journalists. They tell a news story by capturing key images. Like other photojournalists, sports photographers are also artists and craftspeople. They need to capture an image that is fascinating or striking to the eye so that the reader will stop to look more closely. But the image also needs to represent an entire event, scene, or emotion—in one frame. "For years, my recipe for creating great action pictures has been very simple: the best possible composition, light and background to magnify and do the best possible justice to the athlete's performance," says Tristan Shu, who photographs extreme sports.

Sports photography has special challenges too. Bill Frakes, a former staff photographer for *Sports Illustrated*, points out a unique situation sports photographers face. "Color in sports can often be a significant piece of the information puzzle," he said. "For example: Covering a football game at Nebraska where 90,000 people will be wearing red, how could you ignore the color? For me color affects composition, content and mood." In addition, the scenes photographers shoot are often full of action, and the action can be very fast. It helps to know the rules of the game, Frakes said. And if you understand the strategy, you'll be able to anticipate action and set up your shot.

Sports photographers use special lenses that allow them to shoot photos from far away or with a wide angle—such as an entire view of a football or soccer field. They usually have a favorite camera, but they carry a full bag of cameras and other gear with them to events. Longtime sports photographer Peter Read Miller carries four camera bodies and many lenses to every game he shoots. His lenses include telephoto, super telephoto (for capturing details from far away), zoom, and ultrawide zoom (for overall shots). He uses two monopods (like tripods, but with only one leg) to help steady cameras with long, heavy telephoto lenses. He wears a shoulder pouch to hold a lens and a small loupe around his neck to check critical focus—the part of a photograph that is in clear, sharp focus. Because they are trying to shoot players on the field, sports photographers often have to almost lie on the ground in order to see through their cameras.

Frakes says that having all gear in good working condition is one of the most important parts of sports photography. And the make-or-break element of sports photography? "Having complete technical control of your equipment," he says. You have to master your camera before you can master the shot.

"I felt very confident. My team trusted me."

Chastain curled her toes under and fired with the laces of her shoe. This kind of shot is called an instep shot, and it's meant to be powerful but not necessarily accurate. "I didn't hear any noise. I didn't look at [Gao]," she recalled later. "As soon as the whistle blew, I just stepped up and hit it. I just kind of lost my mind."

The goalkeeper Gao read where the shot was going and dived the right way. But Chastain had struck the ball so precisely and with such force, Gao couldn't react in time. The ball flew into the upper right corner of the net, out of Gao's range. The United States had won!

Thunderous applause filled the stadium. Confetti cannons fired, the American team screamed, and Chastain whipped her shirt off. Wearing her black sports bra, she dropped to her knees on the turf, muscles and tendons standing out in clear relief, her white jersey clutched in her upraised fist. She screamed with the sheer joy and triumph of the moment. "Temporary insanity," Chastain said later. "We had been carrying the weight of the World Cup on our shoulders, and this was a release of that weight."

On the sidelines, sports photographers' cameras fired rapid shot after rapid shot. Roberto Schmidt, a photojournalist from Colombia, captured Chastain on her knees—a female athlete with a body like a sculpture, strong, sweaty, triumphant. Magazines and newspapers around the world put the photo on their covers. Long before the thrill of the World Cup was over, Chastain found herself—for a time—the most famous female athlete on Earth.

"We had been carrying the weight of the World Cup on our shoulders, and this was a release of that weight."

Brandi Chastain screamed with joy after her successful penalty kick clinched the World Cup win for the U.S. Women's National Team.

ChapterTwo
OUT OF MANY, ONE

The 20 women who made up the 1999 U.S. National
Team had been as carefully assembled as an intricate
machine—with each person chosen to play her part. Their
journey began in 1986, when the U.S. Women's National
Team was only a year old. Women's soccer had become
widely popular in the United States after the passage of the
federal Title IX law in 1972. Title IX required schools that
received federal money to offer equal sports opportunities
to both boys and girls. For years girls and women had
been offered few, if any, chances to compete equally. With
Title IX and the popularity of soccer for both sexes, that
changed. "In the United States, not only are girls on equal
footing, but the perception now is that American women
can be better than American men," said then-secretary
of Health and Human Services Donna Shalala. "That's a
turning point, a huge breakthrough in perception."

Girls and women swarmed to courts and fields. The year
before Title IX passed, the number of females playing high
school and college sports in the United States was 310,000.
Forty years after its passage, the number had increased
more than tenfold, to nearly 3.4 million. Girls and women
were 40 percent of America's 15 million registered soccer
players by 1991.

The newly formed women's national team needed
a powerhouse leader, and the United States Soccer

Anson Dorrance coached Mia Hamm and many other future soccer stars at the University of North Carolina at Chapel Hill.

Federation (USSF) began to search for a coach. Anson Dorrance applied for the job. Dorrance was already a legend from coaching the men's and women's teams at the University of North Carolina at Chapel Hill. But he had no international coaching experience. The USSF rejected his application. Not qualified, they told him. Dorrance was furious—he wanted that job. The USSF hired Irish-born Mike Ryan, who had coached in the Italian Soccer Federation. But after three losses and a tie in a tournament in Italy with a poorly prepared, badly equipped team, Ryan was fired. Dorrance was in.

Dorrance took a bold approach to managing the team. He cut older players. He sought young, aggressive teenagers with names the fans at the 1999 World Cup years later would recognize: Mia Hamm, Kristine Lilly, Julie Foudy, Joy Fawcett, Carla Overbeck, and Brandi Chastain. He wanted his team to be tough and fiercely competitive. He chose a ferocious captain for the 1986 national team, April Heinrichs. He wanted her to intimidate the team, to make them tougher, and she did. Brandi Chastain remembered trying to steal the ball from Heinrichs during a drill. "I've never been yelled at like she yelled at me. Her face turned bright red. It scared me," Chastain said.

Dorrance believed that women undermine their chances at success on a team by being afraid to compete against their friends. He tried to destroy that kind of thinking by making players face off one-on-one in what he called "Top Gun" drills. He ranked the players after each drill, then posted the results for everyone to see. All of Dorrance's players were naturally competitive. But he wanted the players to forget about whether others on the team liked them. He didn't want them to be nice. He wanted them to be effective.

Team captain April Heinrichs (front) was a fierce player. She would go on to be the first female coach of the U.S. Women's National Team and the first woman elected to the National Soccer Hall of Fame.

The coach had chosen his players carefully. Mia Hamm was a skinny 14 year-old soccer phenomenon when Dorrance went to see her play in Louisiana. Hamm had been obsessed by the game since she was a toddler. When she was not yet 2 years old, she ran up to a man and his son playing soccer in a park. She kicked the ball away from the boy and played with the father for 25 minutes. After that, her life's course was set. The teenager Dorrance saw on the field for the first time was the same one who woke herself up early every summer morning and practiced soccer drills

Mia Hamm (front) has been called the greatest soccer player ever.

alone on a nearby field. Soccer gave Hamm a place in the world, she said as an adult. "Ever since you're old enough to have someone make an impression on you, you're searching for an identity. How do you fit into elementary school, junior high, college? Sports is how I fit in. That was my voice. It made me feel good about myself." Dorrance saw something special in Mia Hamm. He brought her onto the U.S. National Team at the age of 15—the youngest player ever to play at that level.

Midfielder Michelle Akers would play in three World Cups, the first in 1991.

For Michelle Akers, soccer also offered a way out—from an angry, confused childhood and adolescence. Her parents were divorced, and she didn't know how to handle her intense competitiveness. She was drinking and involved with drugs. Soccer gave her a focus away from her troubles. She joined the national team at its very beginning, in 1985. For a while, her life seemed to have turned around. But by the end of 1991, Akers had begun to experience odd physical symptoms—night sweats, headaches, and a deadening, unexplainable exhaustion. She was diagnosed with chronic fatigue syndrome in 1994. Even today the illness is not well understood, and there is no definitive treatment. Sufferers often lose their jobs or their marriages because they cannot function when the disease flares up. They are too exhausted.

Akers manages her illness with a special diet and rest. But her disease can still be debilitating. During the penalty-kick phase of the 1999 World Cup, Akers was not on the field with her teammates. She was in the locker room, getting fluids intravenously to rehydrate after she collapsed on the field.

Chastain, whose nickname was "Hollywood," was more comfortable with fame and celebrity than other members of the team. She smiled easily, was quick to pose with a starstruck young fan, and happily signed autographs. But despite her comfort with the press and her natural flamboyance, Chastain was just as serious about the game as her teammates. Fiercely competitive, she has lived and breathed soccer since she was 6 years old. During her youth soccer days, her grandfather paid her $1 for each goal she made and $1.50 for each assist. Her mother remembers Chastain stepping in to fill a spot on her brother's junior high soccer team. The male players laughed at her, but her brother's team won 6-0. Chastain scored five of the goals. Everyone had stopped laughing by the time the game ended.

Chastain has earned a reputation for almost legendary toughness, grit, and resilience. This is a woman who does

Chastain has earned a reputation for almost legendary toughness, grit, and resilience.

Goalkeeper Briana Scurry (left) collided with Michelle Akers as a tough Chastain (6) battled two Chinese players for the ball in the 1999 World Cup final.

not give up. She had surgery on both knees, and she was dropped from the U.S. soccer roster for four years. She played for a far less prestigious Japanese team half of that time—a comedown some national players might not have accepted. Chastain put her head down and did it.

In 1996 she returned to the U.S. National Team, but she had to give up her front-and-center striker position

Overbeck (left) and Chastain gave their all during the final game and celebrated after winning on penalty kicks.

and move to defense. That same year Chastain played full-time in the Olympic semifinals with a torn right knee ligament. "Brandi's fought through physical and mental battles that would have made others bail out. But she breathes soccer," said her husband, Jerry Smith.

The 1999 World Cup is immortalized in the picture of Brandi Chastain on her knees, but few people other than obsessive fans know that the Cup was almost symbolized

Scurry's dramatic dive blocked a penalty kick by China's Liu Ying.

by another picture—that of goalkeeper Briana Scurry launching herself parallel to the ground to block a penalty kick. The picture is intense—and so is Scurry. The only African-American member of the team, Scurry jokingly called herself "the fly in the milk."

Playing American football was Scurry's childhood love growing up in Minnesota. She liked hitting people legally, she recalled later. Only when her parents felt the game was getting too dangerous for a girl did she drop out. Scurry discovered soccer when she was a preteen. She would watch soccer movies—especially of the great Brazilian star Pelé—and soccer matches around the world

FEW FEMALE SPORTS PHOTOGRAPHERS

Mirja Geh photographed a skydiver jumping out of a plane during a competition in Austria.

Look on the sidelines of any major sports event and you'll see them—the sports photographers, down on one knee, lying on their sides, standing, holding cameras to their faces or peering through cameras mounted on tripods. Now look more closely. Do you notice anything similar about the photographers? That's right—they're mostly, if not all, men.

There are very few female photographers shooting sports. Austrian Mirja Geh is one of them—and one of the few female extreme sports photographers working today. Geh admits that shooting extreme sports can be difficult. In a video presented by Red Bull Illume, a photography competition sponsored by the energy drink, Geh describes shooting with two different cameras while perched on the back of a speeding motorcycle. She also talks about shooting skydivers from a plane so small that it felt lighter when each jumper fell from the open door. She admits that there can be tedium in sports photography too, such as when you are sitting outside in the cold for five or six hours.

Canadian Candice Ward is another one of the few female photographers in sports. She started out both reporting and shooting photos for newspapers in Calgary and Edmonton, Alberta. "I have always loved photography," she says. "I love skipping over the written words and knowing what is going on by looking at a single image." Ward's photos documenting the female football players of the Calgary Rage are powerful and evocative. Each player is posed in the way that Ward feels best captures her spirit. "Doing 32 portraits of these amazing women was definitely a challenge for me, as I did not want them to look like high school portraits or all of them to look the same," she told *Bleacher Report*. "I really wanted to bring something creative to each shoot, but at the same time, shoot quickly."

Sports photography remains primarily a man's profession. But with work like Geh's and Ward's, the sidelines will surely open up to women, just as the field has.

Scurry leaped to make a save during a 1999 semifinal game in Washington, D.C.

on TV. Her father recalls Scurry memorizing moves and practicing faking people out. She was obsessed. In 1989 Scurry's soccer team won the state championship and she was voted Minnesota's top female athlete. Top coaches were taking notice of the goalkeeper as well. At a summer camp for goalkeepers, coach Tony DiCicco told Scurry he was watching her. She promptly let three goals get past her in 15 minutes.

But her nerves didn't get in the way of her success. Scurry was the country's best collegiate goalkeeper by 1993. A week after helping her college team get to the Final Four, Scurry was in training camp with the national team. Dorrance knew a good find when he saw one.

Carla Overbeck (left), Kim Maslin-Kammerdeiner, and Brandi Chastain celebrated a win on their way to capturing the 1991 World Cup.

The women of the national team were a unit. They stuck together. They searched the field—all of them—when a player lost a necklace. When Akers suffered a bout of chronic fatigue syndrome, they drove her home from practice. They were each other's best friends. Their dedication to each other was even spoofed in a Nike commercial in which each teammate, upon hearing that Chastain had had to get two fillings in her teeth, declared that she would also have two fillings.

The team was fierce. The team was powerful. They had won the inaugural Women's World Cup in 1991.

Julie Foudy (11) beat China's Wen Sun to a high ball in the gold-medal match at the 1996 Summer Olympics in Atlanta, Georgia.

And they would not accept anything less than first place again. In 1995 they watched the Norwegian team that had just pounded them 1-0 in the semifinals celebrate with a conga line. They vowed, players and coaches together, that this would never happen again. They would never be anything other than the best.

Their vow proved true. In the 1996 Summer Olympics in Atlanta, women's soccer was included for the first time.

The U.S. National Team played fiercely, taking the gold medal over China. But the Olympics generated more than just medals for the team members—it introduced high-level women's soccer to America. Though the matches were not televised live—a fact that upset many players—the team played in front of tens of thousands of fans. And since Americans have always paid more attention to the Olympics than to the World Cup, the team's win provided the momentum and support to bring the team's World

Members of the U.S. women's soccer team celebrated on the podium after defeating China 2-1 to win the gold medal at the 1996 Olympics.

Tony DiCicco, who coached the women's team from 1994 to 1999, said the players "become sisters, they're all fighting for the same dream."

Cup dreams to fruition. The United States could host a large-scale Women's World Cup in 1999. And it did.

By the 1999 World Cup, Dorrance had resigned. Tony DiCicco was the head coach and was working with women now, not girls. Many of the players were in their late 20s and early 30s—and they knew how to play. What they needed were positive challenges.

As the tournament approached, the women of the U.S. National Team weren't just practicing their best moves on the field. They were also trying to safeguard the future of their sport. They needed to promote the World Cup to an American audience. They needed to promote themselves and women's soccer—in fact, women's athletics as a whole. And they had a vested interest in doing so, because they had a goal that was more important than winning the World Cup. They wanted the same thing that male soccer players had gotten after the 1994 World Cup—the establishment of a women's professional soccer league, just as the men had established Major League Soccer (MLS).

The Women's World Cup board of directors and sponsors Nike, Gatorade, and Adidas managed the World Cup marketing campaign brilliantly. Every game was nationally televised. Commercials celebrating the women were shown during the breaks. Hamm, Chastain, Lilly, Akers, Scurry, Foudy, and others were held up as models of tough, successful female athletes with minds as sharp as their bodies were toned. The campaign worked. Nearly 79,000 fans showed up for the Denmark-U.S. game in New York City. The women had to be escorted off their practice fields by police to keep them from being mobbed by autograph seekers. Fans camped out in the players' hotel lobbies and in the halls outside their hotel rooms. All this for a team that barely played the year after their 1991 World Cup win—the U.S. Soccer Federation couldn't afford to pay them.

Fans around the world were watching the 1999 Women's World Cup. The team was in top shape,

Tiffeny Milbrett (16) fell between two players during hard-fought action in the U.S.'s 3-0 defeat of Denmark in 1999.

well-prepared, and well-coached. Whatever happened in the final game would happen in front of a billion people. Good or bad, it would be remembered forever.

ChapterThree
THE SHOT SEEN ROUND THE WORLD

During the quarterfinal game against Germany in the 1999 World Cup, Brandi Chastain had scored against her own team. The Americans won in the end, 3-2, with Chastain scoring a goal for the U.S. team as well. She was embarrassed when Coach Tony DiCicco, not known for harsh methods, showed a tape of her mistake several times during a team meeting.

But the team wouldn't accept that. They surrounded Chastain and "picked her up," as team captain Carla Overbeck recalled later. Chastain refused to wallow in guilt, and they refused to let her. None of them wanted to do that. By the time they faced China in the final game, Chastain was back. The longer the game lasted, the harder she played. By the end of the overtimes, Chastain was exhausted, like the rest of the team. But also like the rest of the team, she was not daunted.

Many people were on or near that bright, 105-degree field. There were the players, tough, ropy with muscle, ponytailed, sweat-coated. There was the anxious DiCicco, along with Lauren Gregg, his assistant. There were the referees and the fans. And there were people to ensure that the game was documented—the sports photographers. They were on the sidelines, kneeling, standing, sometimes lying on their sides on the ground, giant black cameras held to their faces. Some peered through cameras with huge telephoto lenses mounted on tripods. Briana Scurry pats a

Goalkeeper Scurry comforted Akers after striking her by accident.

stunned Michelle Akers on the back after accidentally hitting her. *Click.* Mia Hamm, her face fixed, her body caught in a frozen moment of athletic grace, dribbles the ball up the field

ahead of a Chinese player. *Click*. Six American players lean forward, faces intent, as they watch Brandi Chastain take the final penalty kick. *Click*.

The photographers were from magazines, newspapers, and news agencies. The Associated Press was there. Getty Images was there. Reuters was there. The French news agency Agence France-Presse (AFP) had sent Roberto Schmidt. It was Schmidt's photo that eventually shot Brandi Chastain into the stratosphere of fame.

Born in Bogota, Colombia, Schmidt had been shooting for AFP since 1989. He was no stranger to photographing war, famine, top political leaders, and important sporting events. His camera has captured images as varied as Sudanese voters trying to register at the polls and a young dancer in India lost in thought. Schmidt, as AFP's chief South Asia photographer, is based in Delhi, India.

Schmidt watched intently, along with the other photographers on the field and the thousands in the stands,

PUBLIC OUTCRY GREETS SELFIE

First lady Michelle Obama (right) sat quietly as British Prime Minister David Cameron (left) posed for a selfie with Danish Prime Minister Helle Thorning-Schmidt and President Barack Obama. The photo went viral on social media.

Roberto Schmidt has only occasionally spoken about the situations behind his photographs, but a photo of President Barack Obama at Nelson Mandela's memorial service prompted a response. Soon after Mandela's celebratory memorial service in December 2013, Schmidt reacted to a public outcry about one of his pictures. It showed Obama in a selfie with two other world leaders—the British and Danish prime ministers—at the service for the former president of South Africa. The three leaders smile merrily for the camera, but first lady Michelle Obama, sitting nearby, gazes sternly off into the distance, seemingly disapproving of the selfie-taking. The public's impression of the photo, which was published worldwide, was that the president, David Cameron, and Helle Thorning-Schmidt were behaving inappropriately at a memorial service. Finally, Roberto Schmidt spoke about the events that were taking place at the moment he snapped the shot:

"I later read on social media that Michelle Obama seemed to be rather peeved on seeing the Danish prime minister take the picture," Schmidt wrote in a blog post. "But photos can lie. In reality, just a few seconds earlier the first lady was herself joking with those around her, Cameron and Schmidt included. Her stern look was captured by chance."

"At the time," Schmidt wrote, "I thought the world leaders were simply acting like human beings, like me and you. I doubt anyone could have remained totally stony faced for the duration of the ceremony, while tens of thousands of people were celebrating in the stadium."

Kicking with her left foot, Chastain drilled the ball into the goal to win the game.

as Chastain set the ball down 12 yards (11 meters) in front of the goal to make the penalty kick. Chastain did not look at Gao, the goalkeeper. She did not want Gao to intimidate her. Earlier in the game, Chastain's legs had cramped up, and she had felt so tired she didn't think she could control her body. But she didn't feel that way now. She was full of adrenaline, and the hormone was doing its job: narrowing her focus to a razor-sharp point, numbing her pain, filling her full of energy. Chastain set the ball down. "Nobody was moving in the stands," Chastain remembered. "I don't think anyone was breathing. I don't think I took a breath."

Gao was a smart goalkeeper—one of the best in the world. But Chastain's blunt, driving, more-force-than-grace kick was so powerful that it was almost in the net before Gao could even spread her hands.

Chastain twirled her jersey in the air after her game-winning penalty kick.

The field exploded with excitement, and Chastain whipped off her jersey and twirled it around her head like a lariat-wielding cowgirl from another time. The cameras'

Roberto Schmidt shot photo after photo, along with the other photographers on the sidelines. History was made.

rapid shots must have blended with the roar of the crowd and the shrieks of the American team. Chastain fell to her knees, threw her head back, and screamed.

Roberto Schmidt shot photo after photo, along with the other photographers on the sidelines. History was made. Schmidt captured Chastain down on her knees. The bright green turf contrasts vividly with the blurry red and yellow of the advertising signs on the stadium walls. Chastain wears a black sports bra, white uniform shorts, white socks, shin guards, and black cleats. Her sweat-dampened blond hair is pulled back in a rough ponytail. The hair around her face is tousled, with loose strands swept back and ruffled around her forehead.

Chastain's hands are clenched and raised in fists. In one hand, she clutches her white jersey top. Her face is contorted in an exuberant yell, her mouth wide open. Her skin is tanned and glistens with sweat. It is hard not to focus on Chastain's sculpted body. The cords stand out on her neck, which is tensed with the force of her yell. Her biceps bulge from her upper arms. Her forearms are sinewy and hard with muscle. The muscles of her bare abdomen are clearly visible. She looks incredibly tough, with the body of an elite athlete—someone whose body is the vehicle that brought her to this success.

There are many, many photographs from that day and that moment. Chastain kneels with her fists upraised, the camera capturing her head-on this time, while behind her, the rest of her team sprints ecstatically across the field. Chastain stands, jersey in hand, leaning back, her

Chastain was ecstatic after her penalty kick clinched a victory for the U.S. team.

stomach as hard and defined as stone. Mia Hamm and
the other players, who had watched from the sidelines,
run onto the field the instant after the kick, their faces

Joyful U.S. players sped onto the field as soon as the winning kick landed in the goal.

split in wide-mouthed ecstatic grins. The laughing and crying players stand in a line with sweat-drenched white uniforms, gold medals around their necks, arms draped over each other's shoulders. They had done it, and this time the whole world had seen.

ChapterFour
ENDURING LEGACIES

"Everything exploded" after the game was over, Brandi Chastain said later. "As soon as the ball hit the net, it all exploded. All the emotion, all the work that had gone into that moment, everyone's anticipation of what the World Cup could be, our satisfaction, it all came together. It was like fireworks. It came out of nowhere."

The win was spectacular. It was one of the great moments in sports, like Roger Bannister's breaking the 4-minute mile, Jackie Robinson's stepping onto the field in a Brooklyn Dodgers uniform, or a young U.S. Olympic hockey team beating the mighty Soviet Union in the Miracle on Ice. Twenty-seven years after Title IX, this Women's World Cup told the world that women's sports had arrived. It inspired people to sit up and take notice. Sportswriters noted that this victory was more than the end of a competition. It was the end of a crusade, to prove that women's sports—and women's soccer in particular—should be taken as seriously as men's.

The team members were celebrated as superstars. They appeared on David Letterman's late-night TV show, visited the White House, and were photographed and surrounded by fans everywhere they went. They were presented to the public as icons of grace, humility, and athleticism— and as role models for young athletes, a label they gladly embraced. "I grew up watching Magic Johnson and Kareem

Twenty-seven years after Title IX, this Women's World Cup told the world that women's sports had arrived.

A triumphant U.S. soccer team celebrated its victory at the Rose Bowl.

Abdul-Jabbar, men I could never emulate. Girls need role models," Julie Foudy said after the win.

The head-on version of Chastain's triumph was

Various photographic versions of Chastain's iconic pose appeared in magazines and newspapers around the world.

splashed on the cover of *Sports Illustrated* with the headline "Yes!" *Newsweek* ran a version of the photo on its cover and proclaimed that "Girls Rule!" Chastain made *SI*'s Year in Pictures.

The choice to publish the photo was not made lightly. Was it appropriate for a role model such as Chastain to take off her shirt? Was it appropriate to print the photo? Almost all photo editors agreed that running the photo was the right decision.

"People made a big deal out of nothing," said Alison Dale, deputy managing editor of photography at the White

> "It was the key moment and celebration photo. To not run it would have been an injustice to the reader."

Plains, New York, *Journal News*. "This is what soccer players do, and this is not the first time she has done this. It is the first time for a lot of people to see because most people do not follow women's sports. Her sports bra covered more of her body than most of the ads we ran daily. Women jog in sports bras everyday. What is the big deal?"

Alan Lessig, a staff photographer at *The Detroit News*, agreed: "My opinion is that there was nothing vulgar or inappropriate about it. She was celebrating her victory the same way we have seen male soccer players do it, by stripping the jersey in a macho way ... why shouldn't she be able to do the same? Her sports bra covered more than we would see at the beach ... or a beach volleyball tournament."

The photo editors generally agreed that their job was to depict the news as accurately and vividly as possible—and that the Chastain photo was the best one to do that. Julie Rogers, weekend picture editor for the *Los Angeles Times*, said, "There actually wasn't a lot of discussion. We decided it was the best image from the game and no one really batted an eye. ... The discussion was that this was the best image. ... I didn't have any reservations about running the picture. It became an important part of the story; she did it in front of a packed stadium and a live television audience. It was the key moment and celebration photo. To not run it would have been an injustice to the reader."

Did they choose the right photo to represent the big

SCHMIDT'S BRUSH WITH DEATH

Buddhist prayer flags fluttered in the wind as a rescue helicopter took off from Mount Everest.

On April 25, 2015, Roberto Schmidt was in an environment very different from the sweltering, colorful soccer stadium of 16 years earlier. He was on Mount Everest, one of the harshest places on Earth: an elemental world of snow, ice, and rock, which tests even the fittest climbers. And that world was about to get even harsher. At noon a massive earthquake struck Nepal. Measuring 7.3 on the Richter scale, the earthquake triggered a massive avalanche on Mount Everest. Tons of snow, ice, and rock thundered down the sides of the mountain, tumbling and crushing people, tents, ropes, and gear in its path. When it was all over, 19 people were dead. It was the deadliest day in the climbing history of the mountain.

Schmidt happened to be there to observe it all—and he lived to tell about it. He wound up buried in a tent, with furniture tumbled on top of him and snow piled up everywhere. Schmidt remembers being in "complete and utter survival mode" and hoping

he wouldn't die. Later he helped evacuate wounded survivors, but he did not ever forget that he was a journalist and that his job was to record the story. As soon as he could find his camera and remove it from the block of ice in which it was encased, Schmidt started shooting pictures again. It was a tricky situation, though. People were hurt, and people were traumatized. Schmidt had to weigh his desire to be sensitive and compassionate against the need to get the story.

It was not easy. He later told *The New York Times*: "You are always torn between helping out or taking pictures. It's a constant conflict. What do you do at that moment? What is your call? I think I'm better at taking pictures than in helping people because that's what I know how to do. It's my job. But if people need help, you help as best as you can. I'm not a doctor, but even a kind word to someone or helping out here or there goes a long way. I think it's possible to do both."

Joy Fawcett's penalty kick sailed by the Chinese goalkeeper. It was one of five successful kicks to seal the victory for the U.S. team.

victory? Chastain's kick won the game, no one would argue about that, but it was only the last of a series of steps that led her to that point. Scurry, the goalkeeper, kept the third-round Chinese penalty kick out of the goal, thus setting up Chastain for the win. Carla Overbeck, Joy Fawcett, Kristine Lilly, and Mia Hamm also scored on their penalty kicks. Michelle Akers played so hard that she suffered from a concussion and dehydration and had to be given IVs in the locker room.

Some argue that the photo is what made Chastain the star of the game, not her actions themselves. Blocking China's third penalty kick, Briana Scurry made a spectacular dive for the ball, stretching herself parallel to the ground. Editors at many newspapers debated whether to use Scurry's photo with their World Cup story or Chastain's. In the end, they went with Chastain's celebratory photo. But if they had chosen Scurry, would she then have been lauded as the star of the game?

Brandi Chastain, soon to be world famous, celebrated with teammates after the winning kick.

Nevertheless, Brandi Chastain became a famous person by any definition of the word. She was the subject of a question on the game show *Who Wants to Be a Millionaire?* She threw out a first pitch at Yankee Stadium. She walked on a fashion runway with Cindy Crawford as her coach, and got a golf lesson from Tiger Woods.

But Chastain was well equipped for the onslaught. "Brandi is attracted to the spotlight like a moth," said her teammate Julie Foudy. "She's a riot, and she's like this Energizer Bunny who never stops."

Her coach agreed. "In many ways Brandi spent her whole life preparing for the last year," DiCicco said. "She always wanted the chance to be a voice for the sport; she just needed that one kick to give her license to do it."

The team had high expectations riding on them. But the lingering aftermath of the win was far from glorious. In a good example of how unequal women's and men's sports still were, each player received a bonus of $50,000 for winning the tournament. That's one-tenth of what a male player would have gotten for winning the Cup.

And the pay differences have not disappeared. The U.S. women who won the 2015 World Cup in spectacular fashion took home $2 million each. That compares with the $9 million every U.S. male player took home after losing in the first round of the 2014 World Cup competition.

The 1999 team faced other challenges, though none that could tear the 20 members apart. Tony DiCicco resigned because of differences with the USSF. There were arguments with the USSF about a victory tour. Nonetheless, the players presented a united front in the negotiations. In the end, the players won and began a two-month victory tour in October 1999. Most of the players continued on with the national team and played at the 2000 Olympics. Some team members retired with injuries or other health problems.

"She always wanted the chance to be a voice for the sport; she just needed that one kick to give her license to do it."

Members of the 2000 Olympic team cheered after making a goal against Norway but lost in overtime 3-2 to take the silver medal. The U.S. Olympic roster of 18 featured 15 players from the 1999 World Cup team.

But the battle with USSF continued. Women on the team continued to protest they were not treated equally with the men's national team. They wanted the creation of a women's professional league. They boycotted a major international tournament and continued fighting USSF until in 2000 the organization offered them significant commitments to developing future players and economic parity with the men's team. In the end, a women's professional league, the Women's United Soccer Association (WUSA), was created. The league played three seasons, until 2003.

None of this affected the feelings the women of the team had for one another. Mia Hamm told a sportswriter, "We'll be great friends until the day we die. We've shared and experienced so much together. And we've grown, too." USSF executive Alan Rothenberg agreed. "They are a unique group," he said. "When you look at what big-time sports is today, they're really a shining light."

Brandi Chastain herself has prospered—in part because of savvy management of her image. She doesn't take part in promotional events that might require removing her shirt. But she hasn't shied from the spotlight. On the contrary, she's enjoyed it and has accepted promotional offers and endorsement contracts worth millions. Along with her teammates, she continued her soccer career, winning Olympic silver in 2000 and gold in 2004. She played professionally in California before becoming a TV soccer commentator.

But Chastain has always been mindful of the path she's paved. In 1999 she told *Newsweek* magazine, "We've had so many moms and kids coming up to us saying, 'You've changed my life and changed the face of women's athletics.' They say, 'You've really changed history.' People ask, 'What type of legacy are you leaving?' I don't believe I can answer that now. ... But I think the greatest impact we'll have is when boys see women athletes and don't think twice about them, just 'Of course girls play sports.'"

And of course American girls and women still play sports, including soccer, very well. The U.S. National Team won the 2015 World Cup in a thrilling 5-2 victory

The U.S. National Team celebrated on the podium in Canada after winning the 2015 World Cup in spectacular fashion.

over defending champion Japan. The U.S. scored four goals in the first 16 minutes of the final game, three coming from Carli Lloyd. The game was played before a crowd of 53,000 in Vancouver, British Columbia, Canada. The U.S. TV audience of 26.7 million was the largest ever for a soccer game, men's or women's.

Next on the agenda? The 2016 Olympics in Brazil, then the 2019 World Cup in France. The legacy of the 1999 World Cup champions continues.

WHERE ARE THEY NOW?

Many players on the 1999 team have stayed within the sports world as coaches, philanthropists, and volunteers. All 20 women were founding members of the Women's United Soccer Association, which lasted three seasons. It was followed by Women's Professional Soccer, a league that also lasted three seasons. Today's National Women's Soccer League is the most successful attempt to establish a U.S. professional women's league. It features national team players from the United States, Canada, and Mexico.

• Midfielder Michelle Akers played in three World Cups and one Olympics. She is a member of the National Soccer Hall of Fame and was named Female Player of the Century by FIFA, the international soccer governing body. She runs a horse rescue program in Georgia that helps mistreated horses find homes.

• Defender and midfielder Brandi Chastain played in three World Cups and three Olympics. She played professionally for the San Jose CyberRays, the Gold Pride, and the California Storm. She lives in California, where she coaches high school soccer teams. She is a co-founder of the Bay Area Women's Sports Initiative, which works with grade school students. She is a leader of the Safer Soccer Initiative to keep heading out of youth soccer. Chastain has worked as a TV commentator.

• Goalkeeper Tracy Noonan (formerly Ducar) was a member of the gold-medal-winning U.S. National Team at the 1998 Goodwill Games. She also played professionally for the Boston Breakers. She was a goalkeeper coach at the University of North Carolina–Greensboro and head soccer coach at Greensboro College. She runs Dynasty Goalkeeping in North Carolina.

• Midfielder Lorrie Fair played on three Olympic teams and played professionally in the United States and Europe. She became the first American to sign with the Women's Premier League in Europe. She is program director for the Charlize Theron Africa Outreach Project and travels internationally for the U.S. State Department's Sports United program.

• Defender Joy Fawcett is a member of the National Soccer Hall of Fame. She retired from the women's national team in 2004 as its highest-scoring defender. She played on four World Cup teams and three Olympic teams. She played professionally for the San Diego Spirit. Fawcett appeared as herself in the 2008 movie *Soccer Mom*. She is a leader of the Safer Soccer Initiative to keep heading out of youth soccer.

• Forward Danielle Fotopoulos holds the NCAA Division I record for soccer goals and points and is a member of the University of Florida Athletic Hall of Fame. She played professionally for the Carolina Courage and then went into coaching at the collegiate level. She coaches women's soccer at Eckerd College in Florida.

• Midfielder Julie Foudy is a member of the National Soccer Hall of Fame. She played on three Olympic teams and four World Cup teams. She played professionally for the San Diego Spirit. Foudy is a co-founder of the Bay Area Women's Sports Initiative, which works with grade school students. She is past president of the Women's Sports Foundation, which advocates for equal opportunities for girls and women in sports. Foudy is a reporter, analyst, and commentator for women's soccer telecasts on ESPN.

• Forward Mia Hamm is a member of the National Soccer Hall of Fame and has been called the greatest U.S. soccer player of all time. She was the youngest member of the U.S. team that won the 1991 World Cup and played on three medal-winning Olympic teams. She serves on the board of directors of the Italian soccer club Roma, in addition to being an owner of the Los Angeles Football Club, which will join Major League Soccer in 2017. She runs TeamFirst, a soccer academy, with Tisha Venturini Hoch and Kristine Lilly.

• Midfielder Kristine Lilly was a member of the national team for 24 years, playing in three Olympics and five World Cups. She is a member of the National Soccer Hall of Fame. Lilly played professionally for the Boston Breakers. She runs TeamFirst, a soccer academy, with Mia Hamm and Tisha Venturini Hoch.

• Midfielder Shannon MacMillan played professionally for the San Diego Spirit and was an assistant soccer coach at UCLA. She won a gold medal with the national team at the 1996 Olympics. She is director of coaching for a southern California youth soccer league.

• Forward Tiffeny Milbrett won medals in two Olympics and played on three World Cup teams. She played professionally for the New York Power and the Gold Pride. She coaches youth soccer in the San Francisco Bay area, is a personal trainer, and hosts women's soccer clinics.

• Defender Carla Overbeck is an assistant women's soccer coach at Duke University, where she has coached since 1992. She played on three World Cup teams and won an Olympic gold medal. Overbeck played professionally for the Carolina Courage. She is a member of the National Soccer Hall of Fame and the North Carolina Sports Hall of Fame.

Members of the World Cup team celebrated on the podium at the Rose Bowl in Pasadena, Calilfornia, in 1999.

• Forward Cindy Parlow Cone played on two World Cup teams and three Olympic teams. She played professionally for the Atlanta Beat and was the first head coach of the Portland Thorns of the National Women's Soccer League. She coaches and directs a youth program in North Carolina. She is a leader of the Safer Soccer Initiative to keep heading out of youth soccer.

• Defender Christie Pearce Rampone, the longtime captain of the women's national team, has played for all three pro leagues. She played for the United States in four Olympics and in five World Cups, including 2015.

• Defender Tiffany Roberts Sahaydak played on three World Cup teams and won an Olympic gold medal. She played professionally before turning to college coaching at Virginia Commonwealth University. She coaches women's soccer at the University of Central Florida.

• Goaltender Briana Scurry played in four World Cups and two Olympics. She overcame a brain injury suffered during a game in 2010, and had brain surgery in 2013. She speaks around the country about the danger of sports concussions and has testified on the subject before Congress.

• Defender Kate Sobrero Markgraf played on three World Cup teams and three Olympic teams. She played professionally for the Boston Breakers and the Chicago Red Stars. She works as a TV soccer analyst.

• Midfielder Tisha Venturini Hoch played in two World Cups and won gold at the 1996 Olympics. She played professionally for the Bay Area/San Jose CyberRays. She runs TeamFirst, a soccer academy, with Mia Hamm and Kristine Lilly.

• Goalkeeper Saskia Webber played professionally for the Philadelphia Charge and the New York Power. She was an assistant coach at North Carolina State University and Rutgers University. She works as a TV commentator and host.

• Midfielder Sara Whalen Hess won a silver medal at the 2000 Olympics and played professionally for the New York Power. She earned a doctoral degree and is a psychologist in Connecticut.

Timeline

1914

The United States Soccer Federation (USSF), then called the United States Football Association, is formed in New York and joins FIFA

1930

The first World Cup takes place in Uruguay

1904

The Federation Internationale de Football Association (FIFA), the international soccer governing body, is formed in Paris

1985

The U.S. Women's National Team plays its first game

1991

The United States beats Norway to win the first women's World Cup

1951

The first U.S. women's soccer league is organized in St. Louis, Missouri

1972

A federal law called Title IX is enacted; it requires that women's sports be given equal attention and money by schools and colleges that receive federal financial support

1977

The first U.S. varsity women's soccer program begins at Brown University in Rhode Island

1996

The U.S. women beat China to win the gold medal at the Olympics in Atlanta, Georgia; it is the first Olympics to include women's soccer

1999

The U.S. Women's National Team beats China to win the World Cup in Los Angeles; the team meets with President Bill Clinton at the White House

Timeline

2001

The Women's United Soccer Association, a professional league, begins play; the league lasts three seasons

2004

The U.S. Women's National Team wins Olympic gold in Athens, Greece, beating Brazil in overtime

2000

The U.S. Women's National Team takes silver at the Olympics in Sydney, Australia, falling to Norway in overtime

2011

The U.S. Women's National Team loses to Japan in the final game of the World Cup in Germany

2012

The U.S. Women's National Team wins Olympic gold in London, England, beating Japan

2008

The U.S. Women's National Team wins Olympic gold in Beijing, China, beating Brazil in overtime

2009

Women's Professional Soccer begins play; the league lasts three seasons

2013

The Women's National Soccer League begins play

2015

The U.S. Women's National Team wins its third World Cup, beating defending champion Japan 5-2 in Vancouver, British Columbia; the popular soccer video game *FIFA 16* includes women's national teams for the first time

Glossary

adrenaline—substance released in the body of a person who is feeling a strong emotion

concussion—an injury to the brain caused by a hard blow to the head or a sudden forceful motion of the head

elite—the best members of a group

exuberant—filled with joyous enthusiasm

forward—team member who plays nearest the opposing team's goal and is most responsible for scoring goals

header—shot in which players use their heads to hit the soccer ball

intravenous (IV)—into a vein

lens—piece of curved glass in a camera that can bend light and focus images

loupe—small magnifying glass

penalty kick—free kick on the goal defended only by the goalkeeper

philanthropist—person who gives time or money to help others

quarterfinals—matches in a tournament that are before the semifinal and final matches

Additional Resources

Further Reading

Christopher, Matt. *Great Americans in Sports: Mia Hamm.*
New York: Little, Brown and Company, 2015.

Downing, Erin. *For Soccer-Crazy Girls Only.*
New York: Feiwel and Friends, 2014.

Hoena, Blake. *Everything Soccer.*
Washington, D.C.: National Geographic Society, 2014.

Internet Sites

Use FactHound to find Internet sites related
to this book. All of the sites on FactHound
have been researched by our staff.

Here's all you do:
Visit *www.facthound.com*
Type in this code: 9780756552930

Critical Thinking Using the Common Core

In Chapter Two the reader learns that Title IX changed the lives of female athletes. Can you imagine a life before Title IX? How is the world different today for women and girls in sports than in the past? Support your answer with evidence from the text. (Key Ideas and Details)

The book begins with a detailed description of part of the final match of the 1999 World Cup. Why does the author choose to open the book this way? (Craft and Structure)

Examine the cover photograph of Brandi Chastain. It is a photograph of a female athlete. But what else does the picture represent to you? Why does it represent those ideas or concepts? Why do you think this picture captured the eyes of the nation so effectively? (Integration of Knowledge and Ideas)

Source Notes

Page 4, line 21: Jere Longman. *The Girls of Summer: The U.S. Women's Soccer Team and How It Changed the World*. New York: HarperCollins, 2000, p. 229.

Page 8, line 2: Ibid., p. 9.

Page 11, col. 1, line 8: DL Cade. "A Day in the Life of Extreme Action/Sports Photographer Tristan Shu." 500px ISO. 3 Aug. 2015. https://iso.500px.com/a-day-in-the-life-of-extreme-actionsports-photographer-tristan-shu

Page 11, col.1, line 16: Zak Bennett. "Q&A with Sports Photographer Bill Frakes." Demotix. 31 May 2013. 3 Aug. 2015. http://www.demotix.com/blog/advice/2104533/qa-sports-photographer-bill-frakes

Page 11, col. 2, line 21: "Q&A with Sports Photographer Bill Frakes."

Page 12, line 1: Bill Saporito. "Flat-Out Fantastic." *Time*. 11 July 1999. 12 Aug 2015. http://content.time.com/time/magazine/article/0,9171,27939,00.html

Page 12, line 5: Mark Starr, Martha Brant, and Sam Register. "It Went Down to the Wire ... and Thrilled Us All." *Newsweek*. 19 July 1999. 12 Aug. 2015. http://web.a.ebscohost.com.proxy.elm4you.org/ehost/detail/detail?vid=8&sid=ef1bb762-08c3-4d21-afd6-16b465bf73d7%40sessionmgr4004&hid=4101&bdata=JnNpdGU9ZWhvc3QtbGl2ZQ%3d%3d#AN=2015494&db=aph

Page 12, line 19: *The Girls of Summer: The U.S. Women's Soccer Team and How It Changed the World*, p. 279.

Page 14, line 12: Ibid., p. 17.

Page 16, line 17: Jere Longman. "For U.S. Soccer Coach, Losing Is Not an Option." *The New York Times*. 30 Sept. 2003. 3 Aug. 2015. http://www.nytimes.com/2003/09/30/sports/soccer/30cup.html

Page 18, line 2: *The Girls of Summer: The U.S. Women's Soccer Team and How It Changed the World*, p.118.

Page 22, line 3: Tim Crothers. "Spectacular Takeoff." 3 July 2000. 4 Aug. 2015. *Sports Illustrated*. http://www.si.com/vault/2000/07/03/283869/spectacular-takeoff-in-the-year-since-her-world-cup-clinching-penalty-kick-went-in-and-her-jersey-came-off-brandi-chastain-has-been-riding-high-enjoying-every-minute-of-her-celebrity

Page 23, line 5: *The Girls of Summer: The U.S. Women's Soccer Team and How It Changed the World*, p. 254.

Page 24, col. 2, lines 4 & 10: Mark Staffieri. "Candice Ward's Ability Behind the Lens Adds Flair to her Sports Photographs." *Bleacher Report*. 9 June 2013. 12 Aug. 2015. http://bleacherreport.com/articles/1663544-candice-wards-ability-behind-the-lens-add-flair-to-her-sports-photographs

Page 29, caption: Nina Mandell. "Former USWNT coach Tony DiCicco weighs in on Hope Solo controversy." *USA Today*. 10 June 2015. 16 Sept. 2015. http://ftw.usatoday.com/2015/06/tony-dicicco-hope-solo

Page 32, line 9: *The Girls of Summer: The U.S. Women's Soccer Team and How It Changed the World*, p. 226.

Page 36, col. 2, line 3: Krissah Thompson. "Roberto Schmidt, POTUS selfie photographer, weighs in on reactions to Michelle Obama." *Washington Post*. 11 Dec. 2013. 12 Aug. 2015. http://www.washingtonpost.com/lifestyle/style/2013/12/11/e9a5adec-6289-11e3-aa81-e1dab1360323_story.html

Page 37, line 9: *The Girls of Summer: The U.S. Women's Soccer Team and How It Changed the World*, p. 278.

Page 42, line 1: Ibid., p. 282.

Page 42, line 25: "Flat-Out Fantastic."

Page 44, line 10: Robert Hanashiro. "The Naked Truth? Comments from photo editors about the Brandi Chastain photo." Sports Shooter: The Online Resource for Sports Photography. 21 July 1999. 4 Aug. 2015. http://www.sportsshooter.com/news/183

Page 45, line 9: Ibid.

Page 45, line 20: Ibid.

Page 46, col. 1, line 19, col. 2, line 12: James Estrin. "On Mount Everest, Surviving an Earthquake and an Avalanche." *The New York Times*. 5 May 2015. 4 Aug. 2015. http://lens.blogs.nytimes.com/2015/05/05/photos-an-earthquake-and-an-avalanche-on-mount-everest/?_r=1#

Page 49, line 9: "Spectacular Takeoff."

Page 50, line 3: Ibid.

Page 52, line 3: Michael Silver. "Playing for Keeps." *Sports Illustrated for Women*. July/August 2001, Vol. 3, Issue 4, p.86.

Page 52, line 5: Ibid.

Page 52, line 19: Brandi Chastain. "A Whole New Ball Game." *Newsweek*. 25 Oct. 1999. 4 Aug. 2015. http://web.b.ebscohost.com.proxy.elm4you.org/ehost/detail/detail?vid=12&sid=3bc589d9-1ca4-4a15-8240-a657b7bb9faa%40sessionmgr113&hid=106&bdata=JnNpdGU9ZWhvc3QtbGl2ZQ%3d%3d#AN=2379627&db=aph

Select Bibliography

Barrabi, Thomas. "Who Is Roberto Schmidt? Photographer Who Captured Obama 'Selfie' Denies First Lady Was Angry; 'Photos Can Lie.'" *International Business Times*. 11 Dec. 2013. 6 Aug. 2015. http://www.ibtimes.com/who-roberto-schmidt-photographer-who-captured-obama-selfie-denies-first-lady-was-angry-photos-can

"Before and After Title IX: Women in Sports." Sunday Review. *The New York Times*. 16 June 2012. 3 Aug. 2015. http://www.nytimes.com/interactive/2012/06/17/opinion/sunday/sundayreview-titleix-timeline.html?_r=2&

Bennett, Zak. "Q&A with Sports Photographer Bill Frakes." Demotix. 31 May 2013. 3 Aug. 2015. http://www.demotix.com/blog/advice/2104533/qa-sports-photographer-bill-frakes

Chastain, Brandi. "A Whole New Ball Game." *Newsweek*. 25 Oct. 1999. Vol. 134, Issue 17, p. 76.

Crothers, Tim. "Spectacular Takeoff." 3 July 2000. 4 Aug. 2015. *Sports Illustrated*. http://www.si.com/vault/2000/07/03/283869/spectacular-takeoff-in-the-year-since-her-world-cup-clinching-penalty-kick-went-in-and-her-jersey-came-off-brandi-chastain-has-been-riding-high-enjoying-every-minute-of-her-celebrity

Estrin, James. "On Mount Everest, Surviving an Earthquake and an Avalanche." *The New York Times*. 5 May 2015. 4 Aug. 2015. http://lens.blogs.nytimes.com/2015/05/05/photos-an-earthquake-and-an-avalanche-on-mount-everest/?_r=1#

"Featured Photojournalist: Roberto Schmidt." *The Guardian*. 15 Dec. 2010. 4 Aug. 2015. http://www.theguardian.com/artanddesign/gallery/2010/dec/08/roberto-schmidt-photography-southern-sudan

Gee, Alison. "Why Women's World Cup Champion Brandi Chastain Bared Her Bra." BBC News. 13 July 2014. 6 Aug. 2015. http://www.bbc.com/news/world-us-canada-27189681

Halloran, John D. "The Rise and Rise of the United States Women's National Team." *Bleacher Report*. 23 April 2013. 6 Aug. 2015. http://bleacherreport.com/articles/1614739-the-rise-and-rise-of-the-united-states-womens-national-team

Hanashiro, Robert. "The Naked Truth? Comments from photo editors about the Brandi Chastain photo." Sports Shooter: The Online Resource for Sports Photography. 21 July 1999. 4 Aug. 2015. http://www.sportsshooter.com/news/183

Joseph, Matthew. "Football: Brandi the toast of the hosts." *The Independent*. 11 July 1999. 6 Aug. 2015. http://www.independent.co.uk/sport/football-brandi-the-toast-of-the-hosts-1105765.html

Kelly, Caitlin. "The Summer That Changed Women's Soccer." *The New Yorker*. 20 Aug. 2013. 6 Aug. 2015. http://www.newyorker.com/news/sporting-scene/the-summer-that-changed-womens-soccer

Lisi, Clemente A. *The U.S. Women's Soccer Team: An American Success Story*. Lanham, Md.: Scarecrow Press, 2013.

Longman, Jere. *The Girls of Summer: The U.S. Women's Soccer Team and How It Changed the World*. New York: HarperCollins, 2000.

McGowan, Tom. "Mia Hamm, the Most Powerful Woman in Football?" CNN. 5 Feb. 2015. 6 Aug. 2015. http://edition.cnn.com/2015/02/05/football/mia-hamm-roma-los-angeles-football-club

Payne, Dave. "America's Cup?" *Soccer Digest*. July 1999. Vol. 22, Issue 2, p. 22.

"Red Bull Illume interviews photographer Mirja Geh about her experiences in action sports photography." ISO 1200 Magazine. 9 Sept. 2012. 6 Aug. 2015. http://www.iso1200.com/2012/09/red-bull-illume-interviews-photographer.html

Saporito, Bill. "Flat-Out Fantastic." *Time*. 11 July 1999. 12 Aug 2015.http://content.time.com/time/magazine/article/0,9171,27939,00.html

Shu, Les. "Essentials: Celebrated Sports Photographer Peter Read Miller On the Gear That Gets the Shot." Digital Trends. 19 Feb. 2013. 3 Aug. 2015. http://www.digitaltrends.com/photography/peter-read-miller-camera-gear

Silver, Michael. "Playing for Keeps." *Sports Illustrated for Women*. July/August 2001, Vol. 3, Issue 4, p. 86.

Smith, Michelle. "What's Brandi Chastain Up to These Days? The Answer May Surprise You." ESPNW. 21 Jan. 2015. 6 Aug. 2015. http://espn.go.com/espnw/news-commentary/article/12203960/brandi-chastain-days-answer-surprise-you

Staffieri, Mark. "Candice Ward's Ability Behind the Lens Adds Flair to her Sports Photographs." *Bleacher Report*. 9 June 2013. 12 Aug. 2015. http://bleacherreport.com/articles/1663544-candice-wards-ability-behind-the-lens-add-flair-to-her-sports-photographs

Starr, Mark, Martha Brant, and Sam Register. "It Went Down to the Wire ... and Thrilled Us All." *Newsweek*. 19 July 1999. 12 Aug. 2015. http://web.a.ebscohost.com.proxy.elm4you.org/ehost/detail/detail?vid=8&sid=ef1bb762-08c3-4d21-afd6-16b465bf73d7%40sessionmgr4004&hid=4101&bdata=JnNpdGU9ZWhvc3QtbGl2ZQ%3d%3d#AN=2015494&db=aph

Thompson, Krissah. "Roberto Schmidt, POTUS selfie photographer, weighs in on reactions to Michelle Obama." *Washington Post*. 11 Dec. 2013. 12 Aug. 2015. http://www.washingtonpost.com/lifestyle/style/2013/12/11/e9a5adec-6289-11e3-aa81-e1dab1360323_story.html

Wahl, Grant. "Out of This World." *Sports Illustrated*. 19 July 1999. 12 Aug. 2015. http://www.si.com/vault/1999/07/19/263721/out-of-this-world-with-the-cup-on-the-line-a-last-second-hunch-and-a-clutch-left-foot-lifted-the-us-to-a-breathtaking-victory-over-china

"Women's Soccer History in the USA: An Overview." American Soccer History Archives. 17 Aug. 2011. 12 Aug. 2015. http://homepages.sover.net/~spectrum/womensoverview.html

Vecsey, Laura. "Briana Scurry handicaps 2015 Women's World Cup field, state of USWNT." FOX Soccer. 7 May 2015. 12 Aug. 2015. http://www.foxsports.com/soccer/story/briana-scurry-handicaps-2015-womens-world-cup-field-state-of-uswnt-050715

Index

About the Author

Emma Carlson Berne has written many historical and biographical books for children and young adults. She lives in Cincinnati, Ohio, with her husband and children.